Illustrated by
Takeo Ishida

Text by

VICTORIA CRENSON

ANIMALS OF THE WORLD

Crescent Books
New York

Copyright © 1973, 1988 by Ottenheimer Publishers, Inc.
Art © 1968, 1971 by Shufunotomo, Tokoyo
This 1988 edition published by Crescent Books,
distributed by Crown Publishers, Inc., 225 Park Avenue South,
New York, New York 10003

CONTENTS

Europe

The **ibex** is a wild goat with long curving horns and a short beard. It lives in the high mountains of Spain and Italy. The sure-footed ibex climbs a steep rocky slope by leaping gracefully from one outcrop to another and tiptoeing along narrow cliffs until it reaches the top.

1

The **red deer** lives in the forests of Europe and Asia. It has a grayish-brown coat that turns reddish-brown in the summer. Like most deer, the red deer eats bark, grass and twigs. Females, called hinds, and their young forage together. Males, called stags, wander the forest alone.

In the early spring, a stag's antlers begin to grow. At first they are just two bumps with a fuzzy covering called velvet. Blood runs through the soft antlers and makes them grow quickly, as much as a half an inch a day! The longer a deer lives, the more points it grows on its antlers each year. By the end of the summer, the antlers are full grown. Now the velvet dries out and peels off as the antlers harden. By rubbing their antlers against trees, the stags scrape off the last tattered pieces of velvet.

During the rutting season in the fall, the forest echoes with the sound of pounding hoofs and loud bellows. It is the stags calling groups of hinds to them. The stag guards his herd. When another stag comes near, the two rivals snort and paw the ground. Then they lock antlers and have a pushing contest that sometimes lasts for hours until one of the stags loses his balance. The winner keeps his herd and mates with the hinds. When the rutting season is over, the stag's battle-scarred antlers fall off. They lay on the forest floor where mice and squirrels eat them, bit by bit, until they are gone.

The **chamois** have hook-shaped horns. They live high in the mountains of Europe and Asia.

Marmots give a loud warning whistle when a predator approaches their burrow.

The **mouflon** is a wild sheep with great, spreading horns that lives on islands off the coast of Italy.

The **elk** of northern Europe is known as the moose in North America.

The **badger's** tidy burrow has many chambers and several entrances.

Fallow deer have coats that are white spotted in summer and grayish-brown in winter.

The **European bison** is extinct in the wild. Less than a thousand captive bison survive in parks and reserves throughout Europe.

The **wild boar** is the ancestor of the domestic pig.

The **lynx** hunts rabbits, birds and small deer in the woodlands of eastern Europe and Asia.

The **European red squirrel** grows bushy ear tufts in the winter.

Reindeer, or caribou, have become the herd animals of the Lapps in northern Norway.

The **roe deer** is common throughout the forests of Europe and Asia.

Africa

The **giraffe** is the tallest animal in the world. From its two-toed hoofs to the tufts on its knobby horns, the brown spotted giraffe stands eighteen feet high. Being tall has advantages for an animal of the African plains. A giraffe can see far across the land and above the tall grasses. It can spot lions and other predators lurking. Shorter herd animals, such as zebras and wildebeest, often join up with groups of giraffe. They know a good lookout when they see one.

When a giraffe sees an attacking lion, it can run at speeds up to thirty-five miles per hour and kick with four very large hoofs. Lions usually do not tangle with fullgrown, healthy giraffes. Instead, the lions work together to bring down young or sick ones.

With its long neck, the giraffe reaches high into the acacia and mimosa trees. It wraps its tongue around a branch and in one motion strips it of leaves, thorns and flowers. The leaves have moisture in them, so the giraffe seldom gets thirsty. When it does, getting a drink can be awkward. The giraffe must spread its legs apart in order to bend over to reach the water.

Male giraffes sometimes fight for mates during the breeding season. The opponents face each other, slap their necks together and crack heads until one of the giraffes becomes so sore that he quits.

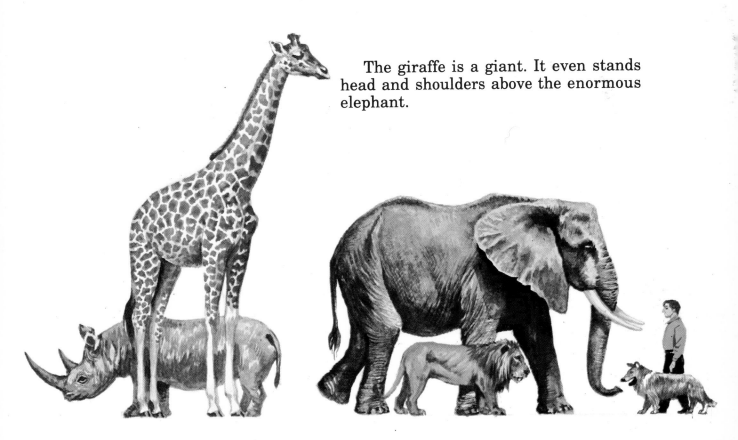

The giraffe is a giant. It even stands head and shoulders above the enormous elephant.

Zebras are wild horses that graze in large herds on the African savannas, feeding on short grass and shoots. The black and white stripes that make them stand out in a group of horses actually help them blend in with the lights and shadows of the grassy plains. Every zebra has a different stripe pattern. That is how zebras recognize each other. All zebras are not black and white. Some are tinged with gray, red or yellow.

There are many hunters who would like to catch a zebra dinner — lions, cheetahs, hyenas and wild dogs. The members of the herd must be alert at all times. That is why when they stop to graze, every zebra turns in a different direction to scan its piece of the horizon for signs of danger. The slightest movement in the grass and all zebras instantly raise their heads. Another rustle and the entire herd takes to its heels, galloping forty-five miles per hour across the African plain.

Horses come in many sizes. From left to right, a pure-bred Arabian, a Shetland pony and a French Percheron.

The earth-shaking roar of the **lion** at dusk on the African plain signals the beginning of the hunt. All day long the "king of the beasts" has rested in the shade. Now with the cool of the evening it is time to eat.

Actually, most of the hunting is done by the females. Lions live in family groups called "prides," made up of one or two male leaders and several females and their cubs.

The hunting lioness creeps up on feeding herds of antelope or zebra and attacks from behind. She leaps on the animal's back and, holding on with her claws, bites the prey through the neck until it suffocates.

When a kill is made, the male lion claims it. When he has eaten his fill, the other members of the pride feed. It may be a week before the pride eats again. That is because the hunt is not always successful. In fact, lions fail to catch their fleet-footed prey more than half the time.

Lions must steal kills from smaller predators or starve. Even though the male does not often hunt for his pride, with his terrifying roar and great maned head he can bully many better hunters from their hard-earned meals and keep himself and his family alive.

The white **rhinoceros** of Africa grows to be six and a half feet high at the shoulders and weigh two tons. On its nose it has two sharp horns. There is no bone supporting the horns. They are really made of hair pressed tightly together to form hard, strong points. The rhino keeps its horns pointed by sharpening them on stones. White rhinos live in small herds and crop the grass with their wide, square mouths. They are peaceful creatures with poor eyesight and hearing. It is easy to get quite close to a white rhino without it noticing your presence.

The black rhinoceros is a different matter. This mean-tempered loner has keen hearing and will charge at the source of any sound it doesn't like, including elephants and cars. It cannot see its victim very well, but it snorts and runs at it anyway, waving its sharp horn. A mother black rhino is especially dangerous when she is protecting her baby.

The spotted **leopard** lives in the forests and savannas of Africa. Leopards range in color from light-colored to black but all have at least faint **spots** showing through their coats. The black leopard is called a panther.

Leopards do not chase their prey. Instead, this cat crouches on a stout branch and waits for an antelope unlucky enough to wander beneath its tree. At the right moment, the leopard pounces on the antelope and bites its throat. Then the strong leopard drags its prey up into a tree where it **can eat** without being disturbed by other predators who might want to steal **the kill**. When it is finished eating, the leopard hangs the carcass on the **branches** and guards it from vultures so that there will be more to eat later. At **night** the leopard roams the forest or plain, climbing trees and attacking baboons as they sleep.

The **chameleon** hides by changing its color to blend in with its surroundings.

The **arui** is a wild sheep of Africa.

The **hyrax** weighs only ten pounds, but it is a relative of the six-ton elephant.

The **serval** lives near swamps and lakes in Africa, where it hunts small game at night.

The **caracal** uses its long legs to jump six feet off the ground and snatch birds from the air.

The **black-backed jackal** eats what is left of lion kills and other carrion.

Sharp-toothed **hyenas** hunt in packs at night.

By living off the fat stored in its hump, the **dromedary** can go a long time without eating.

The **fennec** is a small desert fox that digs its den in the sand.

Cape hunting dogs attack game in a pack and then fight viciously among themselves for a portion of the kill.

Warthogs kneel on their front legs and shovel up roots with their sharp tusks and long snouts.

The **horned buffalo** is pestered by insects. But it has a friend in a bird called the cattle egret. The birds perch on buffalo and pick off the biting insects one by one.

African elephants move across the hot, dusty plains in herds, feeding on grass and leaves and searching for water. Elephants must eat constantly to fuel their huge bodies. They each need thirty to forty gallons of water every day. When watering holes dry up, the elephants use their trunks to sniff the ground for the scent of moisture and then use their tusks to dig down to it.

Male African elephants, called bulls, grow to be eleven feet tall and weigh seven tons. Their enormous tusks are really two front teeth that have grown through the upper lip. The elephant's trunk has a flexible end that works like fingers. With its trunk it can pick up a single blade of grass or tear down branches then stuff them into its mouth. Elephants drink by sucking water through their trunks and squirting it into their mouths.

Elephants are usually peaceful creatures and do not attack unless provoked. But even lions run from an angry seven-ton elephant as it spreads its great ears, coils its trunk out of harm's way and prepares to charge.

The African elephant and the Asian elephant look alike, but side-by-side one can see the differences. An African elephant is larger and has larger ears. The line of its back is less sloping than that of the Asian elephant's. Both male and female African elephants have tusks. Only male Asian elephants have tusks.

The **impala** is an antelope with beautiful, sweeping s-shaped horns. It is an extremely fast runner and can leap ten feet off the ground.

The long-necked **gerenuk** stands on its hind legs to nibble the tender leaves high up in a tree.

Grant's gazelle, like all antelopes, is a swift runner.

Thomson's gazelle is the most common gazelle on the plains of Africa.

The **brindled gnu** is a big-headed antelope that wanders in large herds on the African savanna.

The **oryx** uses its very long, sharp horns to stab its enemies.

The **eland** looks like an ox but is the biggest antelope in the world and weighs nearly a ton.

When two male **sable antelopes** want to see which is the strongest, they kneel down on their front legs and bump each other with their four-foot-long horns.

The male **greater kudu** grows spiraling horns five feet long. These antelopes live in small groups in mountainous areas where they feed on flowers, leaves and grasses.

The **waterbuck** lives near water because it drinks large amounts and eats the juicy grasses that grow near lakes.

The **bongo** is striped so that it can blend in with the undergrowth in thick forests. It is so well camouflaged that it is rarely seen.

Bushbuck rest during the day and come out at night to feed on leaves, shoots and roots in the forests of southern Africa.

The shy **okapi** lives deep in the tropical forest of Zaire in central Africa and is rarely seen. It is the only animal related to the giraffe.

The **hippopotamus** lives in the rivers and lakes of Africa. During the day, herds of hippos float in the water with only their eyes and ears showing. They walk along the bottom churning up mud, then come up every few minutes to breathe or burp and doze. The water keeps them cool. Hippos must stay out of the hot sun or they will die. Glands in the hippo's skin ooze a reddish liquid that works like a sunlotion to protect it from the burning rays of the sun. In the water, the hippo's only enemy is the crocodile. Baby hippos are the crocodile's target, so the babies ride on their mothers' backs.

At night the hippos come out of the water to feed on the grasses by the river bank. Hippos are peaceful plant-eaters, but when threatened by lions, crocodiles or men in boats, the hippo opens its enormous mouth and bites with its sharp, tusklike teeth.

For millions of years, **crocodiles** have lived in the rivers of Africa, waiting for prey to come to the water's edge to drink. As the animal leans over the water, the crocodile lunges and lashes the prey with its strong tail. Then it grabs the animal with its snapping jaws and carries it away. If the animal is large, the crocodile stuffs it beneath a log or rock underwater until it is soft enough to swallow whole.

Unlike the lion or the leopard, the **cheetah** does not have strong jaws, big teeth or any other special killing power. It depends on speed. The cheetah is the fastest animal on land. It chases down antelope or ostrich at speeds of seventy-five miles per hour. But the cheetah can only run this fast for a short distance before it gets tired. It must catch its prey in the first seconds of the chase or quit. Cheetahs are not fighters. Other predators find it easy to bully a cheetah off its kill.

Some of the speeds reached by animals
(expressed in miles per hour)

Elephant 25

Giraffe 32

Greyhound 40

Horse 42

Hare 45

Gazelle 50

Cheetah 75

Chimpanzees live on the edges of tropical forests and on the plains of central and west Africa. These intelligent apes live in noisy groups led by the noisiest male. They feed on leaves, insects, eggs and sometimes kill for meat.

The **gorilla** is the largest and most ferocious-looking ape. But in fact, it is a shy, gentle animal that eats only vegetables and fruits. When a gorilla howls and beats its chest, it is trying to scare away its enemy so that it will not have to fight. Illegal hunting of the gorilla has put this peace-loving ape in danger of extinction.

▼

The **mandrill** is a colorful ▶ monkey with a bright red nose, blue cheeks and an orange beard. Mandrills feed on the ground during the day and climb trees to sleep at night.

The **ring-
tailed lemur**
lives in the
mountains of
Madagascar,
an island off
the west coast
of Africa.

The **guereza** leaps from tree
to tree and rarely comes
down to the ground.

Guinea baboons live in large groups in which
each baboon holds a certain rank. If the group
is attacked, all the male baboons fight back.

Mono monkeys use
shrieks and other
sounds to tell each other
about intruders.

The **sacred baboon** was used as the model for
the face of the Sphinx built by ancient
Egyptians.

29

Asia

For centuries people have captured and trained the **Asian elephant** to do heavy work. The elephants knock down trees and carry logs with their trunks to clear land for planting. They carry people safely through jungles and the tall grasslands of tiger country. The gentle Asian elephant has even been trained to perform in circuses.

In the wild, the Asian elephants live in family groups of ten or twenty elephants with an older female leading the herd. Whether they live in the forest or grassland, the herds travel in single file with the female leader in front. If a predator should try to attack the young, the elephants stand shoulder to shoulder in front of the young and form a protective wall. The leader will charge the predator if she has to.

Tigers live in all sorts of climates from cold, snow-covered Siberia to the steamy jungles of Indonesia, in swamps, grassland and in the mountains. They can grow to be ten feet long and weigh 600 pounds. Stripes <u>camouflage</u> the big cats in the lights and shadows of the brush so that they can approach prey without being seen.

A tiger has a large hunting territory of up to 400 miles that it patrols constantly. Throughout its territory, a tiger has several lairs, such as a rock crevice or shady thicket where it returns to rest and to eat its kills. Heat bothers tigers so they often cool off in a river or stream. Tigers are excellent swimmers.

The **leopard** lives in forests and on the wooded plains of Asia and Africa. The color of its spotted coat varies from gray to yellow depending on where it lives. But no matter what the background color, the clusters of spots called "rosettes" are always there. Even the black leopard, or panther, has spots showing through its coat.

Because their coats are so beautiful, leopards have been hunted and killed for their skins. Others were hunted because they killed livestock. Now there are not many leopards left.

A relative of the leopard is the very rare **clouded leopard**. It is a small, short-legged cat that lives in tropical forests. The clouded leopard hides in a tree and pounces on rabbits or birds that pass below.

The twenty-foot-long **Indian python** kills by wrapping itself around large prey and tightening its hold until the victim cannot breathe.

The **slow loris** of southern India moves slowly through the trees at night, eating insects and lizards.

The **arna** is the wild buffalo of India. Its horns spread six feet across.

The **Malayan tapir** is a nocturnal animal that lives in tropical forests where it feeds on plants.

The **Indian mongoose** is so quick that it can kill a poisonous cobra before it strikes.

Blackbucks live in herds in dry woodlands in India. Each herd is led by a male who marks his territory during the mating season by rubbing trees with a scent from special glands on his face.

The **chital** of India and Sri Lanka is a reddish-brown deer whose enemies are tigers and leopards.

The **sambar** is a large deer of southeast Asia that has a mane and three-pointed antlers that grow to be four feet long.

The **Indian porcupine** climbs trees at night to eat bark and leaves.

The **Indian rhinoceros** has only one horn. Poachers kill the rhinos then sell their horns to superstitious people who believe the horns have magical powers.

37

The **gibbon** is a small ape that lives in the jungles of southeast Asia. It uses its long arms to travel quickly through the jungle by swinging hand over hand through the trees. Another name for these nimble apes is "tree walkers."

Gibbons are very intelligent animals. They live in noisy family groups of male, female and young. The male gibbon spends much of his time defending his territory from other gibbon families.

The **orangutan** is a large, gentle ape with soft, reddish-brown hair. It lives only in the forests of Borneo and Sumatra. Orangutans are aboreal creatures. That means they spend all their time in the trees and rarely come down to the ground.

Orangutan means "old man of the woods." Male orangutans live alone. They do not fight each other for territory or mates. Mothers and their young stay together only until the babies are grown. These long-haired apes are rare. Their numbers have become even smaller because people shoot mother orangutans in order to capture their babies and send them to zoos.

For many years people thought **wolves** were vicious killers that would attack humans and eat them. In fact, a healthy wolf has never attacked a human.

Scientists who study wolf behavior have found that wolves live in close-knit family groups. The group, or pack, includes a leader wolf and its mate, several adults who do not breed, and a litter of pups. The pack hunts together, plays together and all members help to take care of the young. Wolves greet their leader affectionately by wagging their tails and licking his face, then howling together.

Even working together, wolves have a hard time catching large game. They are only able to bring down sick or injured animals. Destroying the weak leaves more food for the healthy animals in a herd. In this way, wolves actually strengthen the herd of animals they prey upon.

Most of the time wolves survive by eating small animals such as rats, lemmings or rabbits.

Wolves are the largest member of the dog family. In the far north, Inuit (Eskimos) have bred their dogs with wolves to get bigger, stronger sled dogs.

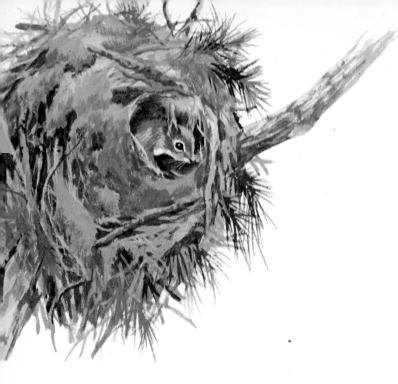

The **red squirrel** lives in the forests of Europe and Asia. Its coat is a different color depending on where it lives. Squirrels in Asia are grayer than the reddish ones of Europe. But they all have white chests.

Red squirrels eat fruit, mushrooms, buds and bark, but their favorite foods are the seeds of pine, spruce and fir trees. The busy red squirrel is a nimble tree climber. It uses its bushy tail for balance as it scurries along branches collecting food to store for winter. As winter approaches, the squirrel grows long tufts of fur on the tips of its ears.

High in the treetops, the red squirrel builds round nests of sticks and covers them with leaves and moss. Here it keeps warm during the cold winter months and raises its young in the early spring.

The **Siberian chipmunk** must survive harsh winters when food is scarce and temperatures are below zero. It digs a tunnel two feet long with underground chambers for storing seeds and mushrooms, as well as a sleeping chamber. When the wind turns cold, the chipmunk crawls down the tunnel and curls up in its grass-lined burrow to sleep. Throughout the winter the chipmunk wakes up from time to time to nibble on the seeds it so cleverly stored.

▼

The **Siberian tiger** is the biggest cat in the world. It grows to be nine feet long and weigh 600 pounds. Siberian tigers live high in the mountains where it is very cold. Their thick, shaggy coats keep them warm.

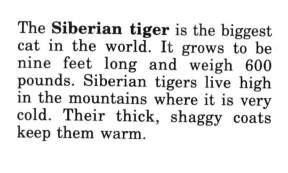

The **sable** belongs to the weasel family. It has always been valued for its dark, glossy fur. Once close to extinction, the sable is now protected by the Soviet government.

The **flying squirrel** is a nocturnal animal that glides from tree to tree.

The **marmal** is a huge red deer that stands four and a half feet at the shoulder.

The playful **otter** lives in a den tunneled into the side of a river bank.

The **brown bears** of Asia grow to be quite large and weigh more than 1700 pounds. Like the brown bears in North America, these bears are usually vegetarians but sometimes catch fish or kill small animals for meat.

The **red fox** is a clever hunter and eats anything that it can catch, such as mice, rabbits and birds. Fox babies are called "kits."

The **Asiatic black bear** is found in forests in Pakistan, India, China and the Soviet Union. It is smaller than the brown bear and weighs up to 330 pounds. It is recognized by its black fur and white "v" collar.

The **Sika deer** lives in the woodlands of China, Japan and Korea.

The stoat or **ermine** is a large weasel that lives in northern woodlands. The ermine is a nocturnal animal. That means that it is active at night. At dusk the ermine comes out of its burrow and hunts rats, mice and birds, raids a nest for eggs, or catches fish. This weasel is a good climber and swimmer.

During the summer the ermine's coat is brown. In winter it changes to white so that the small game hunter can blend into the snowy background.

The **serow** is an antelope that lives in the mountainous areas of India, China and Burma. It lives alone or in small groups. Each serow stakes out its grazing territory by marking trees and the ground with a strong-smelling liquid. The liquid comes from special glands in front of the antelope's eyes and between its toes.

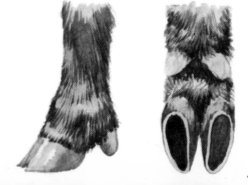

The **snow leopard** lives high in the mountains of China and Tibet where it is very cold. Its tail is three feet long with spiky fur. Hairy cushions on its wide paws keep the cat from sinking in deep snow. Its thick fur coat is pale gray with black spots that camouflage it in the snow-covered, gray rocks.

The snow leopard hides on rocky ledges and leaps upon prey that pass by

— deer and wild goats, such as the ibex. In winter, the game animals move down the slopes of the mountains where it is warmer. The snow leopard follows and spends the winter in the thick forests. In spring the snow leopards move higher into the mountains. The female makes her den in a rock crevice and lines it with her own fur. There she bears two or three cubs that stay with their mother for more than a year.

The **giant panda** lives in the mountainous forests of China. It is a nocturnal animal and feeds all night on bamboo shoots. The giant panda uses its front paws to hold its food because it has a thumb! Although it has poor eyesight, the giant panda has a keen sense of hearing.

The giant panda looks like a bear, but because of many unbearlike traits, scientists put it in a class of its own. Now there are new tests that show that the makeup of the giant panda's genes are closer to a bear's than scientists first thought.

The **red panda** looks like a cross between a raccoon and a red fox. It lives in hilly forests of Nepal and China. Like the giant panda, the red panda feeds at night on bamboo shoots as well as other leaves and roots and an occasional bird's egg.

Red pandas clean themselves like cats do, by licking their fur. It drinks by dipping its paw in the water and then licking it.

The **Himalayan tahr** lives high in the cold mountains. It has a thick, shaggy coat to keep it warm. Tahr graze early in the morning and again at dusk. During the day, they stay well hidden.

The **markhor** is a large, mountain-climbing goat that lives in the Himalayas and in Afghanistan. Its remarkable horns spiral outward and grow to be four feet long on males.

The **musk deer** is a tiny deer that does not grow antlers. But the male deer does grow two long, pointed teeth that look like tusks.

The **argali** is a wild sheep with tremendous curling horns five feet long. It lives in the dry regions of Siberia and Tibet.

The **Siberian ibex** often climbs all the way to the top of a mountain as it grazes, and down the other side.

The **sloth bear** of India and Sri Lanka eats ants, but its favorite food is honey.

The **yak** is well suited to the steep slopes and cold temperatures of the mountains of Tibet. In spite of its bulky appearance, the yak is agile and a good climber. Its thick fur protects it from the cold, cutting wind. Yaks have long been herded by the people of Tibet.

53

Although most of the **Bactrian camels** have been domesticated, there are still a few hundred wild camels living on the Gobi Desert. The two-humped camel likes a cold, dry climate. It eats dry, scrubby plants and drinks very little water. Its broad feet are ideal for rough terrain. A thick, shaggy coat keeps the camel warm.

The **saiga** is a medium-sized antelope that lives on the steppes of the Soviet Union. The male has slightly curving horns. The saiga has a fat nose that works to keep out the blowing sand of the steppes.

The **great jerboa** looks like a combination of a kangaroo, a mouse and a rabbit. It is a desert animal that hides in a cool, underground burrow during the heat of the day. At night it comes out to hop about and look for food.

Przewalsky's horse is the wild horse of Asia. It stands about four and a half feet at the shoulder and has a stiff, dark mane. Faint stripes on the horse's back and legs resemble a zebra's stripes. Only a few remaining Przewalsky's horses roam the plains of western Mongolia.

The **bobac marmot** lives high in the mountains of central Asia.

The **isabelline** bear lives in the Himalayas.

The **Asiatic wild ass** lives on the desert plains. It eats dry grasses and needs little water to survive.

Australia

Many of the animals of Australia are found nowhere else in the world. It is the home of animals with pouches called marsupials and egg-laying mammals called monotremes.

The **koala** is a slow-moving marsupial, or pouched animal. It lives in eucalyptus trees and eats only leaves from this kind of tree. During the day koalas prop themselves in a fork of the eucalyptus tree and sleep. At night they open their large eyes and begin to feed.

The eucalyptus is an evergreen tree with strong-scented oil and acid in its leaves that can be poisonous to a koala if it eats too much. That is why koalas sniff each leaf before they munch.

When a baby koala is born it is tiny and pink. It crawls through the mother's fur to her pouch where it latches onto a nipple and nurses. For six months the baby koala grows inside the pouch until it is too big to fit. Then the young koala hangs onto its mother's back and begins feeding on leaves.

Hunters once found that koalas were easy targets when they were asleep in the trees. They shot them in great numbers until there were few left. Now koalas are protected by law.

The **kangaroo** is also a marsupial. A baby kangaroo, called a "joey," grows in its mother's pouch. At six months old, the joey sometimes hops out of the pouch to play. If there is danger, the joey jumps back into the safety of the pouch and its mother leaps away. A kangaroo's hind legs are very strong. It can travel as much as forty-four feet in one hop.

The **tree kangaroo** is also a good hopper, but it spends most of its time feeding and sleeping in the trees.

The **sugar glider** has furry skin stretched between its ankles and wrists. It leaps from a high tree and spreads these furry wings to glide to up to 150 feet to another tree.

The **rock wallaby** lives in caves and among boulders. It has rough foot pads that keep it from slipping on smooth stone.

The **cuscus** is a slow-moving opossum that lives in the trees. It sleeps during the day and climbs about at night, feeding on leaves and fruit.

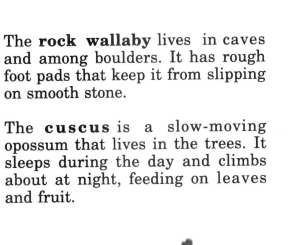

The **thylacine** hunts wallabies, rats and birds. It moves on all fours but when frightened, it hops away quickly on its hind legs like a kangaroo. The thylacine has a backward-facing pouch to carry its babies.

The **platypus** is a very confusing animal. It has webbed feet and a ducklike bill, a flat tail like a beaver and the body of an otter. It lays eggs and nurses its young.

North America

The **polar bear** is the largest meat-eating land mammal in the world. Standing on its hind legs, an adult stands ten feet high and weighs as much as 1,000 pounds. Its yellowish-white fur blends in with the snow and ice of the Arctic region where it hunts.

During the summer, polar bears eat small animals, berries and birds' eggs. But in the winter, polar bears head for frozen bays, where ice floes form, to hunt seals. The polar bear does not chase seals through the water. Seals are much too fast. Also, there are killer whales who would enjoy a meal of polar bear meat. Instead, the polar bear finds a hole in the ice where the seals come up to breathe. It waits patiently for a seal to surface and then grabs the seal with its claws and throws it onto the ice. The stunned seal is then easy prey for the hungry polar bear.

Polar bears wander and hunt alone. They only form pairs during the mating season. As winter approaches the female stays on land and uses her sharp claws to dig a den in the snow and ice. There she sleeps and lives off her body fat until spring. Her cubs are born in December. She nurses them until mother and cubs come out of the den in April.

Caribou, or reindeer, travel in herds. They must always keep moving to find food in the arctic regions where they live. During the winter, caribou wander along the edges of the snowy north woods eating lichen, called reindeer moss, that they uncover with their shovel-shaped antlers.

In the spring when the snow melts, grasses, moss and flowers are plentiful on the tundra to the north. The small caribou herds gather in great herds and migrate 600 miles to the north to graze. The caribou swim across rivers and lakes to the treeless tundra. The land is very soggy but the caribou's wide feet keep them from sinking in the mud.

Here millions of biting insects are more than a nuisance. Their biting sometimes drive the caribou to panic. Baby caribou are often trampled as the caribou race about trying to escape the clouds of insects. When chilly autumn arrives, the insects disappear and leave the caribou in peace. With the first snow, the enormous herds migrate again to the southern edge of the tundra where the forest offers reindeer moss and protection from the cold wintry blasts.

The **musk ox** lives on the frozen arctic tundra of Canada and Greenland. It stands five feet tall at the shoulder and can weigh up to 700 pounds. When wolves threaten a herd, the musk ox form a circle around their young and keep the wolves away with their horns.

The **arctic hare** grows a thick, white coat in winter to camouflage it and keep it warm.

Greenland lemmings are rodents that feed on lichens, grasses and moss.

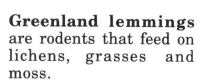

The **arctic fox** also changes its coat. In winter it is white. In summer it is light brown and then turns a bluish-gray.

The **Kodiak bear** of Alaska is nine feet tall when it stands on its hind legs. It is the largest brown bear. Like other bears, the Kodiak eats berries, buds, leaves, honey and insects. It also kills birds, fish and big game such as deer.

When a brown bear comes out of its den in the spring, it is very hungry. All winter long it has lived off the fat in its body. Now it must eat a lot to regain its weight and to build up its store of fat for the next winter's sleep. Hungry male bears will even attack a mother bear to take her new cubs. When they do, the mother bear fights to the death to protect her young.

The **wolverine** lives and hunts alone. This four-foot-long weasel is fearless. It will even attack a moose and try to kill it with sharp claws and teeth. Wolverines patrol their hunting territories, stealing prey from other predators who might trespass on it.

When explorers and settlers came to North America, they discovered **beaver** dams on every stream. Trappers who traded in the thick beaver furs sent millions of skins to hatmakers in Europe. As beaver became more scarce in the east, trappers headed west and north to find them, exploring much of the country along the waterways. Settlers followed them, clearing land for farms and building villages. You could say that the country was opened up because of the energetic beaver.

Beavers spend much of their lives swimming in cold water and they are well adapted for it. They paddle through the water with webbed hind feet and steer with their flat tails. Special flaps close over their ears and nostrils to keep water out when they dive. A beaver can stay underwater for nearly fifteen minutes. Keeping warm is important for the beaver, so it has two fur coats. The undercoat is thick and oily to keep water away from the beaver's skin.

Beavers build dome-shaped homes called lodges in the middle of ponds. Each lodge has two underwater entrances and an underwater storeroom where the beavers store bark and twigs to eat during the winter months. They make these small ponds by building dams across streams. Using their long, orange teeth to gnaw down trees along the banks of the stream, the beavers float the trees into position and add mud and sticks to hold back the water. The strong dams keep the water at just the right level to cover the lodge entrances.

The **bighorn sheep** lives in the mountains of western North America, feeding on the grasses in high mountain pastures. The male bighorn has thick curving horns with deep ridges. The female also has horns, but they are not as long or as tightly curled as the male's.

Bighorns graze in large flocks. Each flock has a leader who must always prove his strength. Other males challenge him to head crashing contests. For hours or sometimes days, two bighorn sheep, with heads lowered, charge each other again and again, banging their hard heads together with loud cracks that echo from the mountainsides. The contest is only over when one of the bighorns gives in.

Bighorns can keep their balance on the steepest slopes and narrowest rock ledges because their feet have special pads that grip the smooth rock. A bighorn can leap from one side of a deep gorge to the other and never lose its footing.

The **mountain goat** lives above the timberline in the Rocky Mountains. Near the snowy mountain peaks it is very cold. The mountain goat's thick, shaggy fur keeps it warm. Like the bighorn sheep, the mountain goat has special pads on the bottoms of its hoofs that grip the bare rocks. It is so sure-footed that it appears to run straight up the side of a cliff. Mountain goats graze in mountain meadows in small flocks or alone.

The **moose** is the largest deer in the world. It stands almost six and a half feet at the shoulder. Its antlers are enormous, almost four feet wide.

Moose feed in marshes, bogs and lakes where they eat water plants and shoots. They are excellent swimmers and often dive to the bottom of lakes for their favorite food — water lily roots. In winter the moose eat twigs from willow and aspen trees.

Except for mothers and calves, moose live alone. When one becomes old or sick, the large creature is prey to bears and wolves. Because they are so large and strong, it takes the cooperation and cunning of a whole pack of wolves to bring down even a sick moose.

A **timber wolf** pack hunts the game that enters its territory. The wolves urinate around the boundaries of their territory. The scent tells outsider wolves that they are not welcome. Each wolf has a rank in the pack. A leader wolf and its mate are the only ones who have pups. The other wolves live by the decisions the leader makes. There is rarely any fighting among members of a wolf pack.

The **grizzly bear** is omnivorous. That means that it eats roots and grass shoots and also hunts moose calves and fawns. But its favorite food is probably salmon.

Each year at the end of the summer, great numbers of salmon swim from the sea upstream to spawn and lay their eggs. Grizzly bears line up along the streams to fish for them. Defending a good fishing spot often leads to battles between bears.

Among grizzlies there are different fishing styles. Some bears stand in the shallow water and quickly pin the fish to the bottom with their big paws. Some dive for fish and try to catch them with their jaws. Others find it easier to just steal another bear's catch. The bears eat many salmon and build up the reserve of fat they will need to survive the long winter hibernation.

The **black bear** lives in the woodlands of North America. It eats anything it can find — berries and roots, insects and honey. Once in a while it does kill for meat.

Black bears do not hibernate. They sleep on and off during the winter, coming out on milder days. During the winter cubs are born. They are quite small and blind at birth, but by the time spring comes, they are ready to roam with their mother.

Mother bears are very protective of their cubs. A mother bear will charge and fight any creature that she believes might harm them. For two years the cubs stay with their mother, learning to find food and avoid danger.

The **wapiti** gets its name from the Shawnee Indian word meaning "light rump." These large deer live in herds. Males gather in separate groups from the females and young. During migrations, the small herds come together in big herds of more than a thousand deer. The wapiti follow the food supply. In winter when food is scarce in high mountain areas, the wapiti move together down to valleys and plains to browse on bark and twigs.

The **white-tailed deer** lives in forests and swamps throughout North America and some parts of South America. When a predator approaches, the deer makes its escape through the forest. It flashes the white underside of its tail as a warning flag to all other deer in the area to say, "Danger nearby."

Females, called does, have one to three fawns in the spring. The fawns are light brown and covered with white spots. To keep her babies safe, the doe hides them in the undergrowth. Their spotted coats blend in with the dappled sunlight on the forest floor. The fawns sit very still, invisible to anyone who passes. These new babies also have very little scent so predators cannot track them. The doe stays a distance from her young so she will not lead enemies to them. In a few months, when they are strong enough, the fawns join their mother to look for food in the forest.